uinoa #nofr ▮▮▮▮▮▮▮ #v

✔ KT-475-485

st #slowbarista #AGA
gistdelay #scattercushi
cketsquare #wheresmy
eal #almondmilk #ipad
mycleanersname #toon
atagdisaster #plasticch
syforyoga #ineedagav
dom #burntmyquinoa #
ell #nutritionalyeast #s
oforganic #dermatolog
gh #coconutwater #stai
#paleofail #thestruggl
contrast #guacomolein
lidays #johnlewiscrisis
ampagneglass #toomu

MIDDLE CLASS PROBLEMS

REAL PROBLEMS, BUT NOT REAL ACTUAL PROBLEMS, JUST MIDDLE CLASS ONES

BENJAMIN LEE

Illustrations by Matt Blease

◩ SQUARE PEG

Published by Square Peg 2014

4 6 8 10 9 7 5

Copyright © Benjamin Lee
Illustrations by Matt Blease © Square Peg
Designed by The Curved House

Benjamin Lee has asserted his rights under the Copyright, Designs and
Patents Act 1988 to be identified as the author of this work

First published in Great Britain in 2014 by Square Peg
Random House, 20 Vauxhall Bridge Road, London SW1V 2SA

www.vintage-books.co.uk

A Penguin Random House company

A CIP catalogue record for this book is available from the British Library

ISBN 9780224101127

Every effort has been made to credit the authors of these tweets.
Please contact the publishers with any corrections.

Penguin Random House is committed to a sustainable future for our
business, our readers and our planet. This book is made from Forest
Stewardship Council® certified paper.

Printed and bound in Italy by L.E.G.O. S.p.A.

#CONTENTS

#INTRODUCTION

Even as you read this introduction, you're probably going through a whole host of middle class problems yourself. I bet that John Lewis sofa is covered in a few too many scatter cushions. I'm guessing that you probably put a little bit too much hand cream on just before you started reading and your fingers are a little oily. I imagine that you might have a stray piece of dill stuck in your teeth and it just won't budge.

If this sounds like a regular day in your troubled life, then the good news is you're not alone.

The bad news is that you've forgotten to buy quinoa for your dinner party tonight.

Since 2010, I've been following the lives of the middle classes on Twitter, highlighting the many plights suffered on a daily basis. For the first time, in this book you're holding, I've collected the best examples of how frightfully inconvenient things can get.

#EATING IN

When it comes to eating in, there's an Aga-sized gap between expectations and reality.

Your ideal self would never have forgotten that extra lemon or accidentally singed that Fortnum & Mason tea towel with the crème brûlée blowtorch...

Softly weeping against your Fisher & Paykel fridge is essentially your only option

I think I've given myself
a croissant headache.

@michfreeman 12:22 PM – 3 Oct

Lemon & lime yoghurt.
I was right to be
sceptical.

@CahirMcD 1:16 PM – 11 Mar

Cooked dinner too long in the slow cooker though. Should've made it when I got home. Broccoli is destroyed. #notblessed

@Kyle_Peabody 12:50 AM – 9 May

I BOUGHT GREEN OLIVES TODAY, FOR A MEAL WITH FRIENDS TONIGHT, INSTEAD OF BLACK. I CAN'T THINK OF ANYTHING THAT'S GONE THIS WRONG FOR AGES.

@saramca 4:55 PM – 30 May

There's nothing worse than a burnt brownie, sigh #overcooked #baking

@soriko 12:24 PM – 3 Jun

Made falafel. No longer want falafel. Sigh.

@BadPenfold 7:30 PM – 23 Mar

Accidentally roasted cucumber instead of courgette. Terrible.

WTF I can't find my melon baller! :'(

I was eating some madeleine cake the other day when, in a sudden rush, it came to me that I've never read any Proust. #getsmeeverytime

@ashdavidson 4:51 PM – 12 Oct

Really want to pig out but no food in house. Forced to feast on quorn burgers and yoghurt. #notquitethesame

@MartinAnge 8:51 PM – 24 Nov

Do I really need to keep three different types of balsamic vinegar?

@TastyChefsWife 11:49 AM – 4 Jun

It took me far too long
to discover pesto

@jwheare 12:27 PM – 3 May

I HATE developing biscuit recipes. Keep going wrong. One batch so bad, it ended up in the bin :-(

@catlilycooks 2:48 PM – 13 May

Jesus Christ making risotto is really boring

@JessieRatkinson 10:00 PM – 16 May

"

I CAN'T BELIEVE I
BOUGHT A TOASTER
WITH FUCKING PAGE
SE THIRD...

"

@peter_watts 9:23 AM – 23 Mar

Cut my thumb whilst julienning a green papaya. Oh the perils of cookery!

@RachelSwanny 2:58 PM – 7 May

Oh no I forgot to drizzle a tbsp of manuka honey over my breakfast!

@McTristram 10:04 AM – 18 Feb

Oh dear, it was my fault the Le Creuset oven dish dropped and cracked. It's totally broken now. :(

@BeCoffin 6:07 PM – 16 Jun

I'VE HAD THIS AVOCADO FOR 3 WEEKS THAT SIMPLY WON'T RIPEN. WHAT SHOULD I DO WITH IT? CHUCK IT OUT THE WINDOW?

@TeaBrat 11:42 PM – 2 Jul

MY DOG ATE MY CAVIAR #OffTothePound

I wish there was a restaurant that delivered foie gras

put too much balsamic vinegar on my salad and now im dying

@IonaEJ 2:06 PM – 28 Apr

I've eaten too many M&S croutons on an empty stomach and now I feel sick. #milddisaster

@Annemcx 7:38 PM – 14 Mar

And there is no butter left for my scone. This is an absolute nightmare.

@_Cr4zy_Fool 10:31 AM – 2 Aug

I generally feel guilty
about neglecting to use
my juicer as much
as I should

@charlieluf 12:08 PM – 28 Jul

Damn, I've added too
much water to the
couscous. This is a
catastrophe! #dinner

@GuyPortman 7:37 PM – 4 Aug

"YOGHURT COATED SESAME SNAP CONSUMPTION BECOMING PROBLEMATIC"

@umop_3pisdn_ 5:00 PM – 28 Jun

Honestly you lot,
I thought the same
as you. I don't WANT
to have discovered
there's such a thing as
too much Halloumi.

Sadly, there is.

@ned_potter 7:03 PM – 26 Feb

Catching up on Masterchef. Wasn't it a bit unfair when one team had wild turbot, asparagus and morels & the other had guinea fowl & kale?

@StewyB 8:58 PM – 9 May

#EATING OUT

Going out for dinner sounds fun on paper: exactly what you need after a strenuous day at work (enough with the LinkedIn invites already).

But it's never quite the blissful escape you imagine.

You booked online but of course, you have to wait 15 minutes for your table and by the time you've finally sat down, there are at least three dishes you'd gladly order and deciding between them is giving you a headache, not helped by that glass of sauvignon blanc, which, frankly, is on the warm side.

———————

My sister accidentally spilt wasabi in my green tea ice cream and now I'm fucked

@Thatsbraandun 3:16 AM – 22 Apr

To the food festival where they ran out of Nepalese goat curry.
I am bereft.

@scaryduck 2:45 PM – 25 May

My sushi is all
stuck together
:-(

"

I ALWAYS PUT
WAY TOO MANY
TOPPINGS IN MY
FROZEN YOGHURT
AND NEVER GET
TO ENJOY THEM
IT ALWAYS FROYO
MELTS BEFORE
I CAN

"

@frnchvanila 10:39 PM – 4 Jun

This Greek salad is good but half of it is all feta cheese #toomuch

Arghhh wasabi burn. My sinuscs are on fire.

I don't think I've ever put the actual amount of salt I want on my food.

@McDowellCharlie 3:15 PM – 10 Apr

I need some 1:1 tuition about mussels. I don't understand them.

@Maya00003 11:11 AM – 22 Jun

I'm currently bemoaning the fact that they brought my tea at same time as my goulash despite request for goulash to follow in 15 minutes.

@ToonLawyer 11:25 AM – 20 Feb

A SWAN JUST SPAT
IN OUR SALSA.

@gothick 3:28 PM – 31 Mar

How did I have to tell
an Italian restaurant
to dice the tomatoes
on my bruschetta??
They litts have made
tomatoes on toast

@hannnahboorman 4:15 PM – 9 Jan

Too much truffle oil
gives me a headache :'-(

@tavypreap 1:35 AM – 12 May

Seriously, how hard is it to poach an egg properly? #disappointing #breakfast

@vickyariches 11:24 AM – 5 Jan

Forgot to take a photo before demolishing my frozen yogurt.

@graylola 8:56 PM – 5 Jul

Why's the chocolate on Pret choc chip cookies always so damn melty? It's both a blessing and a

CURSE

@Chevychased 1:46 PM – 17 Jan

the cafe cut my sammich in a rectangular shape rather than the preferred triangular configuration. i can tell this week is going to be awful

@shutupadie 10:30 AM – 30 Jun

So I've forgot to buy crisps for lunch & I've mixed my cordials. Safe to say I don't want to live in this world anymore.

@rhyswynne 1:16 PM – 21 Jul

Why would anyone ever ruin a sandwich with this many black olives? It's blasphemy

@SambamRivera 6:30 PM – 26 Jul

#SHOPPING

Given that the home delivery option has betrayed you one too many times (what kind of animal replaces satsumas with clementines?), trekking to the local supermarket remains the most reliable option for stocking up the kitchen/pantry/guest house.

But nowhere are you safe from small-scale catastrophe, not even in the free-from organic aisle or in the soft-furnishings section of your favourite department store.

Am I the only person who gets to the supermarket and has to sit in the car for 20 minutes gathering the strength to go in?

@SaraThornton1 12:25 PM – 4 Oct

Accidentally bought
red pepper humous
instead of sweet chilli.
#dayruined

@t4mmyp 1:23 PM – 9 May

I need a new wallet
because I have too
many cards ! >(

@qabyqirl 3:48 PM – 1 May

No lemongrass,
no coriander, no ginger,
no prawns in @waitrose
#unacceptable
I live in Surbiton.
Not Beirut.

@S77MNF 5:36 PM – 30 Jun

"

I WANNA ORDER
A DESK FROM IKEA
BUT IM ALWAYS
BUSY SO I WON'T
BE HOME TO SIGN
FOR IT WHEN ITS
DELIVERED. #SMH

"

@CameronTerez 6:48 PM – 20 Jun

Ironic that today is the "longest day". It always feels like that when I go to IKEA.

This classics degree malarkey has really messed up my amazon recommendations

@naomijoy10 12:25 AM – 21 Jun

MY WALLET IS TOO SMALL.

@Hussainjef 6:11 PM – 27 May

My new tv is awesome.

Is what I'd be saying if Panasonic provided me with 4 x M6 bolts to attach it to my stand with.

Too much to ask.

@markyboyace 4:17 PM – 8 Jan

I hate food shopping,
freezer aisles are
always so cold🖐❄

@kllyblfr 7:23 PM – 26 Jun

JUST REALISED THE ALMOND MILK I BOUGHT HAS SUGAR IN :'(

@marchingstars 8:24 AM – 10 Mar

*Help me put the
shopping away
I said, I now can't
find anything...*

Forgot to buy more
certified organic gluten
free wraps today how
depressing lol

@veganlifee 8:52 AM – 29 Mar

#QUINOA

REPEAT AFTER ME

KEEN-WAH*

*QUINOA

Need i say more?

I've been saying quinoa wrong all this time. The shame.

@d_cornish 5:55 PM – 8 Jul

Woman in the works canteen couldn't pronounce quinoa properly. I HATE HER

@Hendoballs 9:13 PM – 8 Oct

Paleo fail this morning. Forgot to put quinoa in slow cooker last nite & paleo muffins were mouldy. Gave up & had porridge before my run.

@Pipssqueaks 6:41 AM – 26 Oct

GOT INTO A HEATED ARGUMENT WITH MY SISTER OVER HOW TO PROPERLY PRONOUNCE QUINOA.

@ashleysprout 2:51 AM – 29 Jul

Like eating quinoa.
Hate cleaning it up
after cooking.

@neil_burnside 8:38 PM – 10 Apr

I made quinoa and
cashew burgers and
forgot to take pics
(>_<)

@AmidstTheCrowd 3:33 AM – 23 Jun

Just dropped batteries in my quinoa this is weird even 4 me

@EllieDoh 2:03 AM – 15 Jun

breakfast was disappointing. Never had quinoa before and don't think I'm ever likely to again.

@sehenderson 9:26 AM – 15 Aug

> *Wow just dropped my quinoa salad on the library floor... Fuck*

@KatannahHolden 4:51 PM – 16 Jun

Have you seen the price
of Quinoa these days?

@Gillian 5:18 PM – 6 Aug

I'm so sick of the word
quinoa. It's everywhere!

@cidneyverdell 12:38 AM – 12 Jun

#DRINKING

Adequate hydration is a basic
human right.

Try telling that to the barista who seems
utterly incapable of understanding
the words "extra foam".

I dislike ordering
'2 cappuccinos'
which sounds oafish.
'2 cappuccini' sounds
pretentious. Usually
ask for 'A cappuccino..
oh actually two'

@DeeChris 12:18 PM – 30 Nov

Just ordered a flat white with Soya milk. It's vile. What do I do?!

@miabubble 2:15 PM – 16 Jul

This is the worst chai latte I've ever had the displeasure of consuming.

@callmekatrepp 3:01 PM – 28 Jul

NO.... I DO NOT WANT MY MACCHIATO FILLING TO THE TOP WITH FOAM... THAT WOULD MAKE IT A CAPPUCCINO

@annapriceless 12:22 AM – 10 Mar

ugh i always forget to make my tall skinny vanilla latte extra hot!!!! (lmao if i was my barista i'd hate me)

@georgiatraylor 12:07 PM – 22 Apr

This tea selection
isn't exotic enough

Starbucks is so
incredibly noisy.

Smashed my favourite
champagne flute.
Nightmare.

@Quoink 6:18 PM – 18 May

So mad that there's no more raspberry tea bc now I'm stuck w either pomegranate or orange cinnamon and both are repulsive

@ElaPoplawski 3:33 AM – 12 Jun

That moment when you crave an Old Fashioned and don't have any Bitters to hand. And the shops are shut. That.

@V2VFP 2:30 PM – 20 Apr

I just drank my Berocca too early and got a mouthful of orange foamy fizz.

@aklettner 1:38 PM – 6 Mar

There are people
spitting at my
champagne tasting
class #sacrilege

Secretly want to cry
when I run out of
almond milk. . .

I'm dying w/o my daily ginger shot.... I cant believe our juicer broke!

I feel betrayed when the water dispenser refuses to work on my fridge...

OH GOD THEY'VE STOPPED SELLING MY FAVOURITE NESPRESSO CAPSULE.

@marcooth 10:51 AM – 5 Jul

I want a massive
sugary coffee but I
don't trust myself
with the cafetiere.

Large coffees are
never large enough.
What a cruel world.

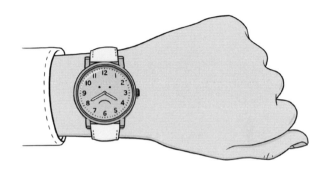

NOTHING BOTHERS ME MORE THAN A SLOW BARISTA

@LZeee 9:38 PM – 23 Jun

You get home to do some work and open a bottle of Rioja to help... and it's corked. Cruel cruel world.

@PaulFulford 8:33 PM – 1 May

#WORK

The fact that you even have to work
is an indignity in itself.

And since you don't yet have a driver
you're forced to drive yourself, or, even
worse, face the crowds in some form of
crudely assembled metal torture chamber
for a seemingly endless journey.

How **are** you supposed to concentrate
on the latest Murakami?

Once you finally get to work, not only has
the cleaner done a shabby job of the office
but that conference call comes through
five minutes earlier than planned, which
means you don't even have enough time to
get your assistant to fetch you a chai latte.

You might as well be down a mine.

Ran out of @YorkshireTea at work, and now had to resort to PG Tips..... #whatadowngrade

@Deejay_Ra 12:59 PM – 18 Jan

Toughest part of my job today: Picking a PowerPoint theme/ design! Gr.

@HeatherInNVan 12:28 AM – 1 Feb

I have so many poems to type up I'm just way too lazy

@__SweetLullaby 3:08 AM – 22 Jun

In our London office
we have chefs who
make our lunch.

In our Amsterdam office
we get given ingredients
to make sandwiches.

I miss London.

@gpb1979 12:00 PM – 24 Apr

**WHENEVER I WRITE
'ADVOCACY' IN
LAW MY HANDS
AUTOMATICALLY
START WRITING
'AVOCADO' AND
IT IS BECOMING A
REAL PROBLEM.**

@jxssiejxckson 6:29 PM – 7 May

Too many awards
ceremonies I was bound
to miss one ... #whoops

I am literally crying at
work because I didn't get
any Kate Bush tickets.

Chelsea super busy with the flower show... Just want to get home!

JUST FOUND OUT IT'S POSSIBLE TO OPT OUT OF THE COMPANY-WIDE BIRTHDAY CAKE AND SING-SONG TRADITION. I'VE BEEN HERE TWO YEARS. LIVID.

@MollieMcGuigan 12:59 PM – 7 Jan

THE NEW GUY AT THE OFFICE IS FAR FAR FAR TOO FRIENDLY

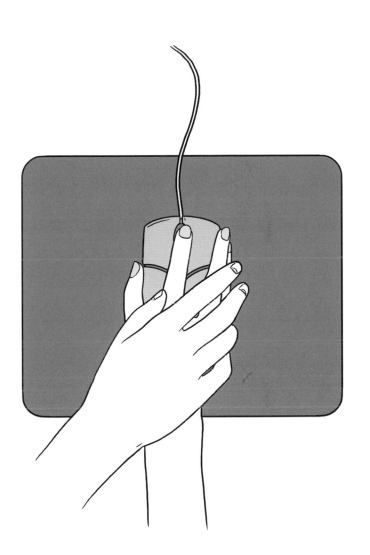

Suffering from writer's block.

@Moe 4:18 PM – 21 May

#TECHNOLOGY

Right now, you're thankful that what you're holding is a book. You don't need to charge it or update the firmware or furiously scream voice commands, you just need to turn the pages.

Because, quite frankly, you crave the simplicity of your youth, not this sci-fi novel you're now living in.

A leisurely drive in the car has become a tense struggle with the satnav.

A conversation with a friend has turned into a desperate battle to stop taking pictures of your hands with your phone.

And that damn iPad, the one with bulgur wheat stuck to the screen? It's practically possessed.

Almost spilled hummus on my iPad. Almost...

@Miss_Kim_H 2:00 AM – 20 Mar

Wasabi pea stuck to kindle cover

@simonplotkin 1:09 PM – 26 Sep

Gawd. Sometimes my phone doesn't recognise my thumb and I have to manually swipe and tap in a whole four digit code. Jeez.

@CarolynWillitts 6:42 PM – 30 May

I NEVER THOUGHT
I'D HEAR THESE
WORDS COME
OUTTA MY MOUTH,
BUT I THINK MY
TV IS TOO BIG

@willieboy1978 11:32 AM – 17 Jun

GAH! iPhone Twitter app is the WORST! All my drafts gone for the 2nd time. Half-crafted puns that'll never see the light of day. I weep.

@quovixi 12:48 PM – 17 Apr

Having to delete photos for making room in your phone is like having to kill some of your children because you cant feed them all

@HebaAlDuwaisan 2:00 PM – 23 May

Have not been able to send a single iMessage all day. Have had to force them all to go as SMS.

@drgitlin 6:29 PM – 1 Oct

Just tried to plug my phone charger into my iced cappuccino. How's your day going?

The buffer speed of 4OD is driving me to alcohol

I wish I had a name I could actually use for my twitter username. Alexandria Annelaine is just too damn long.

@callie_oop 3:18 AM – 16 May

WhatsApp always seems to go down whenever I'm waiting for an important reply... How do I send a normal text message again?

@Furqan_Naeem 9:17 PM – 8 Jun

A non-wifi bus.
In 2014. Where
are we; Siberia?

@AlwynPayne 8:07 AM – 9 Jan

**THERE IS ALMOST
NOTHING WORSE
THAN RUNNING
MICROSOFT EXCEL
ON A MAC. WORST.
EXPERIENCE. EVER.
ALL. THE TIME.**

@hrbrmstr 8:09 PM – 9 Oct

Is there a way I can hack my Kindle so it just GOES BLANK? I want it to rest when I am. It stresses me out every time I look at it.

@anna_ee 7:06 PM – 20 Mar

spent an hour googling "how does 3D printing work" and I JUST DONT UNDERSTAND #mindblown #help

@legiorno 10:31 PM – 3 Jan

TOO MANY BUTTONS IN THE NEW CAR THOUGHT I'D PRESSED THE SUN ROOF BUTTON BUT I'VE PUT ON PARKING SENSORS AND CAN'T TURN THEM OFF

@_laurenteresa 3:36 PM – 5 Aug

"

LEARNING JAVA
WITH NO PREVIOUS
PROGRAMMING
EXPERIENCE IS
TOUGH

"

@samnorth1 10:37 PM – 9 Aug

Susan spilled iced tea all over my kindle. The pages of my real life books will collect my tears.

@tphoebs 11:15 PM – Jan 20

Car key remote is broken. Have to manually lock the doors with the key, like some sort god damn barbarian.

@TomCullen 6:47 PM – Jun 19

#CHRISTMAS

Scrooge was severely misunderstood.

Christmas is hard.

———————

Dear expensive wrapping-paper makers. If it's too thick to fold and Sellotape doesn't stick to it, it's not really wrapping paper is it? Grr

@marcusfairs 11:07 PM

I JUST SPENT $15 ON THE WORST "CHRISTMAS COOKIE SCENTED" CANDLE EVER AND THIS IS WHY I HAVE TRUST ISSUES

@ohmyyrikk 4:42 AM – 3 Dec

I've heard the kettle boil
3 times now and not
once have I been brought
a cup of tea. WORST
CHRISTMAS EVER.

@Whitepawprint 9:03 AM – 25 Dec

FEEL LIKE I SHOULD GO SHOPPING TODAY BECAUSE THERE IS SOOO MUCH ON SALE. FEELING GUILTY THAT I'M NOT!!

@Mobelline 1:30 PM – 26 Dec

I hate wrapping presents for kids because they don't appreciate the craftsmanship behind gift wrapping

@thebookfellow 11:42 PM

My parents' wifi can't cope with all of our devices. This is the worst Christmas ever. Twelfth attempt at sending this...

@Donna_Gallers 9:23 PM – 25 Dec

#THE HELP

If Dostoyevsky were living in Primrose Hill today it's pretty likely that he would be writing about this, one of the keenest sources of middle class angst of our time:

Getting stuck in the house at the same time as the cleaner.

Can never quite relax
when the cleaners
around the house

@Barney1044 3:09 PM – 14 Jul

Cleaning lady is
upstairs and she's
being way too loud :/

@jasmineelaine_ 11:38 PM – 9 Apr

CAR WON'T BLOODY START SO IT LOOKS LIKE I'M STUCK AT HOME WITH THE CLEANER TODAY #GETOUTOFMYHOUSE

@janeseymour94 12:06 PM – 23 Jan

That awkward moment when you let the housekeeper come in and clean your room while you sit in front of your laptop and work. :)

@HornIT 5:35 PM – 24 Oct

Yes gardener, please continue your loud garden maintenance.

Yikes, it's find a new au pair time...

If I could pick one thing for the cleaner not to have hidden, I think my aeropress might have been it. Am about to smash kitchen apart.

Just been informed that our cleaner isn't coming today, which means I panic-tidied my room at 1am for NOTHING.

@siankhunter 11:19 AM – 4 Jul

OK THIS IS NOW THE 4TH TIME THE LADY WHO DOES MY IRONING AND DRY CLEANING HAS COME 3 DAYS LATE AT A TIME I'M NOT IN. GONA HAVE TO LET HER GO

@daisymaycarter 12:23 PM – 13 Feb

That ironing lady has shrunk all my clothes

Texting the ironing lady on behalf of the husband and adding kisses by mistake. #fauxpas

Our ironing lady has
deserted us :-(

@Nushi_B 7:16 AM – 16 Jun

My gardener obviously thought the world was ending, hence him buggering off and leave my sprinkler on for 5hrs.

@Catboy92 11:09 AM – 21 May

#AT HOME

While it's difficult to feel at ease in the outside world, a place of mispriced Nespresso capsules and hellishly overcrowded artisan bakeries, your home should be a haven from the daily ordeal.

But even here you're not safe: the damn humidifier keeps making that weird noise, making it almost impossible for you to hear "The Archers", which is having a bit of an off week anyway, to be honest. You can't even spend time in the conservatory without desperately wishing there was space for another wicker chair.

It never ends.

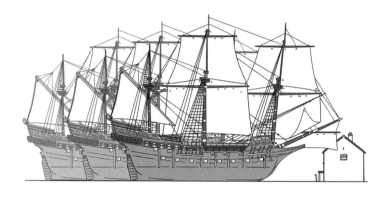

We now have three boats in the driveway. I realise how this sounds but it's frightfully inconvenient

@Jazzleberry 4:51 PM – 22 Dec

Dreamt we found a Fabergé Egg in Granny's attic. Never woken up more disappointed!

@samuelsawalker 7:33 AM – 8 Apr

Too many good tv shows and not enough time to watch them all

@RoblesAntonella 6:16 AM – 19 Jun

"

I'VE HAD THE
THEME TUNE
FROM THE ARCHERS
STUCK IN MY HEAD
FOR ALMOST TWO
WEEKS. SEND HELP.

"

@mikegrady87 9:08 AM – 24 Jan

That Moment When You Realize That You Are Wearing The Wrong Pair Of Slippers -_-

Ripped my tapestry off the wall to use as a blanket because I'm lazy and cold

*The sodding badgers
have now started
on the celeriac.*

@NevilleMorley 9:01 PM – 23 Jun

The instructions on how to descale a Nespresso machine are among the least comprehensible things I've encountered

@ChrisMonk 3:00 PM – 14 Jun

Anybody else in Harrogate whose cat is being terrorised by an owl?

Can only assume owlets around.

@crablanevets 8:06 AM – 26 Jun

JUST TOLD MY DAD OFF FOR HAVING HIS OPERA TUNES TOO LOUD AND I FEEL BAD FOR HOW UPSET HE SOUNDED WHEN HE OBLIGED

Awake at 5am and searching for #wedding venues, I thought this was going to be the easy part #fussy

@JennyNairPT 7:17 AM – 24 May

So many films to watch, so little time

@HelenaCasson 11:54 PM – 6 Apr

The settings on our new hot tub are testing us... there's only four buttons!!!

@tor861 9:46 PM – 8 May

Feeling emotional watching crufts. Too tired. Actual tears

@Daisy_stophs 8:13 PM – 9 Mar

"

I'M NEARLY
CRYING BECAUSE
I CAN'T FIND MY
THOROUGHLY
MODERN MILLIE
DVD, THIS IS TRAGIC

"

@miss_KT_austen 10:36 AM – 5 Jun

My pug has hiccups.

@darren_scott 8:13 AM – 7 Aug

I hate it when I run out of space on my bulletin board for the pics my kids drew for me, and I have to decide which one to take down.

@mdesjardins 3:52 PM – 14 Sep

MY HORSE JUST ATE MY FAVORITE BOOTS. -_-

I sleep with so many pillows and it gets too hot but its really comfortable so I have a bit of a conundrum

@_allessejones 1:01 AM – 23 Jul

#ON HOLIDAY

Finally, the one time of year when you're allowed to relax.

But before you've even stepped anywhere near a plane, you're starting to stress out. What if the first class lounge is busy again? What if the hotel only serves scrambled eggs, not poached? What kind of holiday would that be?

IT'S A BIT GUSTY IN CANNES.

@wendyide 2:37 PM – 13 May

*Feel like I've
forgotten how to ski*

ONE TIME I WATCHED A MOVIE IN SPANISH WITHOUT SUBTITLES ON A PLANE

@maplemacchiato 10.36 AM – 2 July

I HOPE THIS YACHT HAS WIFI

@BESTDEATH 5:58 PM – 15 Feb

I didn't just leave my heart in San Francisco – I also left my @Dior sunglasses

@socialsteffie 4:14 PM – 5 May

Shitty WiFi at hotel.
Borrow LAN cable
to see if it's faster.
Realise Macbook Pro
doesn't have a slot
for LAN cables.

@ViperChill 11:27 AM – 27 Jun

I am going to New Zealand tomorrow and I am SO UNPREPARED

@fancypanther 9:43 AM – 4 Jul

I'm being forced to play croquet I hate my family

@cleopayne99 11:50 PM – 25 Jul

"

SO THE WIFI
IN FIRST CLASS
DOESN'T EVEN
WORK, AND
THE FREE CUP
OF TEA WAS
DISAPPOINTING
TO BE HONEST
#IWANTAREFUND

"

@lauren_chasey 9:30 PM – 27 Dec

> *Need to have words with my hotel room cleaner. She keep changing the toilet roll so it's the wrong way around.*

@Welshside 10:26 PM – 3 Jul

DARLING, WE HAVE A PROBLEM...

**PACKING LIGHTLY
IS TOO HARD**

@MissAnnaRose1 12:45 PM – 25 Jun

New batch of people
have arrived at the
hotel. They're noisy and
splashy in the pool.

@matthew_white 12:17 PM – 30 Jun

Packing to go away
is the worst.

@chrissybrigden 9:00 AM – 1 Aug

After 48 hours, just worked out how to properly use the shower in the hotel.

@John_murphy1 4:51 PM – 28 Jul

Vacation problem:
I am sick of ceviche.

@AlyssaNewcomb 8:57 PM – 5 Jun

I need a holiday
to recover from
my holiday

@JessBatten 4:55 PM – 21 Apr

#LOOKING GOOD

While all else crumbles around you, it's important that at least you look your best. So even when the dog walker/ flute teacher/ latin tutor is running late, again, you can feel safe in the knowledge that aesthetically, you're a winner.

That is, until your facialist takes yet another holiday, your yoga mat goes missing, you shrink your cashmere jumper in the wash, and your personal trainer goes through a particularly angry phase.

It's just too much. You're having a spa day and that's final. If you could just work out the damn online booking form...

Broke my hair clip
getting into a Jaguar.

need hand cream
DESPERATELY

Omg forgot to
moisturise my legs
AND I ALREADY
LEFT THE HOUSE

most painful
facial ever

NOTHING WORSE THAN REALIZING THAT YOU CUT THE FINGERNAILS ON YOUR LEFT HAND BUT NOT YOUR RIGHT.

@mikesmithwriter 11:00 PM – 6 Feb

Whenever I go to massage therapy I'm always so tired so I can't relax cuz I'm trying too hard not to fall asleep

@A_Mario_Are_I 10:57 PM – 18 Sep

In other news... I now have 3 broken nails. I see 2 hours at the nail salon this weekend. 2 hours!

@Sascja 8:00 PM – 16 Jun

i put a face mask on then forgot about it and it's hardened on my face

i lost my yoga mat what is my life

FIRST EVER YOGA CLASS TONIGHT, WHAT THE FECK SHOULD I WEAR! "SOMETHING LOOSE FITTING"... SHORTS? JOGGING BOTTOMS? GAH!

@Gordon 5:45 PM – 5 Jun

It never fails. The moment I start seriously considering getting a haircut is when my hair starts looking more perfect than ever.

And today I am late because a bus driver wouldn't let me on with my yoga mat. #wtf

@pikelet 7:24 PM – 30 Oct

Hope water aerobics isn't too splashy, it's not a hair wash day

@rayrayk90 6:30 PM – 5 Jun

There's nothing worse than putting on a pair of freshly washed and tumbled dried SKINNY jeans for first time!! Breathe in!
#fashion

@Joanne_Knox 1:23 PM – 3 Jul

I FORGOT MY FRIGGIN EYE MASK. ROOM IS FLOODED WITH LIGHT. WILL NEED A NAP LATER.

@frenchtart 12:44 PM – 14 Jan

Benjamin Lee is editor of Shortlist.com and has written for the *Guardian*. Since 2010 he has run the hugely popular @MiddleClassProb Twitter account.

Matt Blease works as a designer and illustrator for brands including Waitrose, Barbour and the BBC. He has led the Graphic Design team at Liberty, and has a weekly spot in the *Guardian's* G2.

Many thanks to all the long-suffering authors of these tweets. Every effort has been made to credit tweeters; please contact the publishers with any corrections.